UNIVERSITY OF NO
STUDIES IN THE ROMANCE LANG

Number 73

SERMON JOYEUX AND POLEMIC
TWO SIXTEENTH-CENTURY APPLICATIONS OF
THE LEGEND OF THE FIFTEEN SIGNS

SERMON JOYEUX AND POLEMIC

TWO SIXTEENTH-CENTURY APPLICATIONS OF THE LEGEND OF THE FIFTEEN SIGNS

BY

WILLIAM W. HEIST

CHAPEL HILL

THE UNIVERSITY OF NORTH CAROLINA PRESS

DEPÓSITO LEGAL: V. 3.007 - 1968

ARTES GRÁFICAS SOLER, S. A. - JÁVEA, 30 - VALENCIA (8) - 1968

The legend of the Fifteen Signs before the Judgment enjoyed an enormous popularity during the Middle Ages. It seems quite certainly to have originated in Ireland in the tenth century, and thence to have spread to England and the Continent, where it flourished in a number of versions of several easily distinguishable types until the less friendly intellectual climate that developed with the religious changes of the Reformation and Counter-Reformation froze it out. Thereafter it continued to show some vitality, but it survived only at generally lower social and intellectual levels. Its latest recorded appearance, in an incomplete form, was in a German folksong taken down in 1880. But it is safe to say that after the fifteenth century it belongs to folk culture almost exclusively.

At its height the legend was always treated seriously, though it remained a legend, never a matter of official doctrine of the Church. Still, its possible truth was examined by such distinguished Churchmen as Peter Damien, Bruno Astensis, Peter Comestor, Alanus de Insulis, Vincent of Beauvais, and other notables. And it kept its place in such works of piety as homilies and legendaries, and evidently as a sort of familiar landmark in the background of Western Europeans, for nearly a millenium. [1]

Our present interest in this legend is restricted to its place as an item of European intellectual furniture —specifically, of that of Frenchmen— in the sixteenth century. For to that century

---

[1] For a full discussion of the origin and development of the legend, see my monograph, *The Fifteen Signs Before Doomsday* (East Lansing, 1952). For French versions not cited in the monograph, see my articles "Four Old French Versions of the Fifteen Signs Before the Judgment," *Mediaeval Studies*, XV (1953), 184-198, and "The Fifteen Signs Before the Judgement: Further Remarks," *Mediaeval Studies*, XXII (1960), 192-203.

belong two curious works, neither of them very familiar; neither of them of more than slight importance in itself, since both must rank among the lesser works of little-known writers; neither of them very significant in the future course of literature, since neither counts as more than a curiosity after its own century; but both illustrating, in very different ways, the uses that that century might make of its heritage from the Middle Ages. Both appeared as small separate publications, now so extremely rare that in order to discuss them it seems necessary to republish them here. [2] Both refer unmistakably to the legend of the Fifteen Signs in their titles (and one in its text); but neither of them genuinely represents the legend, though the earlier of them does follow the general scheme of the legend in burlesque fashion. And both have titles so similar as to suggest that there must be some special connection between them, though what that may be constitutes a puzzle that I have not been able to solve beyond dispute. Otherwise they differ almost totally in substance, in style, in purpose, and in genre.

The earlier of these pieces has been briefly described by Émile Picot in the second article of his two-part study "Le Monologue dramatique dans l'ancien théatre français." [3] It was entitled, in its earliest edition, *Les Quinze Grans et Merveilleux Signes nouvellement descendus du ciel au pays d'Angleterre* and has been attributed, on the authority of Antoine Du Verdier, to Jean d'Abundance. Virtually all that we know of this writer, other than by inference, comes from Du Verdier's brief notice, the

---

[2] The second seems to have been printed only once, in 1587; and even the better-known works of the author to whom I attribute it were collector's items by 1736: see Niceron's comment, p. 18 below. I know of no surviving copy except that of the Bibliothèque Nationale. The first has been published at least eight times, but only the recent edition by Hugh Shields is at all accessible. Unfortunately, Shields was unable to find a copy of the Silvestre edition. Since the best text was inaccessible to so well documented a scholar as Shields and since the work is quite short, it seems best to make available an edition based upon it. Shields' edition appears in his study "*Les Quinze Signes descendus en Angleterre:* A Medieval Legend in Decline," *French Studies,* XVIII (1964), 112-122. For other editions see pp. 27-30 below.

[3] *Romania,* XV (1886), 358-422, and XVI (1887), 438-542. This piece is discussed in Vol. XVI, pp. 459-462.

content of which has often been repeated, usually with some expansion of wording but little or none of substance. It stands as follows:

"JEAN D'ABUNDANCE. Bazochien & notaire du Pont sainct Esprit a composé plusieurs petits traictez en rime, Assavoir,

"Les quinze grands & merueilleux signes nouuellement descendus du ciel au pais d'Angleterre moult terribles & diuers à ouyr racompter. Item plus la lettre d'Escorniflerie, laquelle porte grands privileges à plusieurs gens. Et la chanson de la grand Gorre. Le tout composé par ledit d'Abundance soubz le nom de maistre Tyburce, demeurant en la ville de Papetourte, & impri. à Lyon sans nom ni datte." [4]

The suggestion that *Jean d'Abundance*, as well as *Maître Tyburce*, is a pseudonym occurs as early as 1773, in a footnote by Rigoley de Juvigny in his edition of Du Verdier: "Ce nom, que Baillet, au nom TYBURCE, dans sa *Liste des Auteurs déguisés*, prend pour un vrai nom, en est un faux, & fait à plaisir. Je conviens que l'Auteur qui l'avoit pris, se l'étoit rendu si propre, que, pour se mieux déguiser, il en inventoit quelquefois d'autres, sous lesquels il se cachoit. Tel est ce nom de Maître Tyburce." [5] Since no evidence is presented in support of this view, I see no reason to accept it. But it has been accepted by Petit de Julleville, [6] by A. Delpy, [7] and by D. H. Carnahan, who has made the fullest study that we have of this writer. [8] Indeed, apparently in desperation from the paucity of records, Carnahan attempts to extract details of the early life of d'Abundance from the surviving titles of two of the writer's lost works, a procedure showing more determination than judgment. [9] The inference that "his use of

---

[4] *La Bibliothèque* (Lyon, 1585), pp. 634-635.

[5] *Les Bibliothèques françoises de la Croix du Maine et de Du Verdier, Sieur de Vauprivas* (Nouv. éd.: Paris, 1772-1773), IV, 325, n. I.

[6] *Les Mystères* (Paris, 1880), I, 337.

[7] *Essai d'une bibliographie spéciale des livres perdus, ignorés, ou connus à l'état d'exemplaire unique*, I, A-G (Paris, 1906), 3.

[8] *Jean d'Abundance: — A Study of His Life and Three of His Works; University of Illinois Bulletin*, Vol. VII, No. 1 — *The University Studies*, Vol. III, No. 5 (Urbana-Champaign, 1906), p. 7 (= p. 225).

[9] *Ibid.*, pp. 8-10.

the word 'Papetourte', in his pseudonym, 'Maître Tyburce, demeurant en la ville de Papetourte', would imply a lack of reverence
for the papal power" [10] surely rests upon a faulty etymology of
the invented name, the first element of which Carnahan evidently
takes to be *pape* 'pope.' But this is certainly the old verb *paper*
"devour, gobble up," and the compound is exactly parallel to
papelard, which is still in use. [11] This name, incidentally, exactly
fits the Land-of-Cockaigne atmosphere of the poem. As Picot
remarks of the signs in this poem, "ce sont les boeufs, les veaux,
les chapons, les comestibles et les boissons de tout genre qui an-
noncent la venue du carnaval," [12] by which he seems to suggest
that the poem, which he classes in the subdivision of *sermons
joyeux* within the general category of dramatic monologues, was
intended for recitation at carnival time. This is likely enough, if
hardly demonstrable. And the list is not nearly so homogeneous
as Picot suggests.

On the strength of the sixth sign (lines 53-56), in which he
sees an allusion to the Italian campaign of François I in 1536,
Picot dates the poem in or about that year. I confess that I do not
see how he extracts this from a rain of Lombards who swept the
French chimneys; but perhaps the last line, "Les Françoys leur
ont fait leur cas," supplies the point. From the evidence of this
and of other works —eight surviving and eleven lost— Picot
suggests that the chief literary activity of Jean d'Abundance took
place between 1540 and 1550, and that though he is said to
have been a notary and *bazochien* of Pont-St.-Esprit —a town now
best known to Americans as the ancestral home of Jacqueline

---

[10] *Ibid.,* p. 11.

[11] It is possible that Carnahan was here misled by Montaiglon, whose
discussion of the writer he quotes (p. 14, n. 1). Montaiglon argues thus:
since " 'maître Tyburce, demeurant en la ville de Papetourte', comme aussi
la grant et vraye pronostication de maistre Tyburce Dyariferos, demeurant
en la ville de Pampelune, est indiquée comme composée en la ville d'Avignon,
il est à croire que nous avons encore affaire à une oeuvre de Jehan d'Abondance." Carnahan does not accept the conclusion, but he may have accepted
the premise, that Avignon is indicated. If so, there are two meanings, with a
pun on *paper* and *pape,* which I doubt.

[12] *Romania,* XVI, 459.

Bouvier Kennedy— his dramatic works, which seem to have been the greatest part of his output, were written for the theater at Lyon.

Our interest in this energetic, versatile, and perhaps under-rated figure —for Carnahan ranks his farce of *La Cornette* with that of *Pathelin* [13]— must here be somewhat restricted, to one of his lesser works, certainly, and one which, if Picot's dating is correct, is that of a prentice hand. It is not, however, a totally atypical work in its outlook or in any essential characteristic. It is the work of an author who has begun to find his native climate, that of the late Middle Ages, a little stifling, but who has never learned to breathe comfortably in any other. Even more than his fellow *bazochien*, Clément Marot, he looks backward more often than ahead, though perhaps he admired Marot for his greater ability to learn the lessons of the new age. We should at any rate be happy to find a copy of one of his lost works, the *Epître sur le bruit du trépas de Clém. Marot*, printed in the year of Marot's death. [14]

Picot speaks loosely when he says, "Les *Quinze Signes* de Jehan d'Abundance n'ont rien de commun avec les quinze signes du jugement dont il est si souvent question au Moyen Age." [15] They have the first part of the title, *Les Quinze Grans et Merveilleux Signes*, in common with many versions of the legend, along with the fact that the signs are enumerated and described *seriatim*. I think, indeed, that we can even identify the type of the legend that d'Abundance is here burlesquing. It would be the type usually designated as the "Old French type," in which marvelous and terrifying falls of things from the sky are pro-minent. [16] Miraculous, though hardly terrifying, rains and snows make up *all* the signs of this sixteenth-century parody. And, like any parody, it depends for its point on the assumption that its audience will be familiar with the original — in this case, as with many of the *sermons joyeux*, a serious, even sacred, original. [17]

---

[13] *Op. cit.*, p. 5.
[14] See Carnahan, *ibid.*, p. 13.
[15] *Romania*, XVI, 459.
[16] This is also the view of Hugh Shields, pp. 113-114.
[17] John A. Yunck, in "The Two Faces of Parody," *Iowa English Yearbook* for Fall, 1963, pp. 29-37, distinguishes between two fundamental varieties

Thus, parodies of the Mass, of various prayers, of wills, of judgments in court, of charters and other legal forms are common. But this is the only work I know that reduces the legend of the Fifteen Signs to buffoonery. And this strikes me as rather characteristically a feature peculiar to its time and place of composition. Of course, the Middle Ages in general, and the *esprit gallois* in particular, had long been capable of jesting with holy things. But in earlier days the Fifteen Signs, though taken seriously enough, hardly enjoyed so high a position among the teachings or formulae of the Church as to constitute a suitable subject for burlesque. As the hold of the legend weakened further, I surmise, the distinction between it and the genuinely sacred became blurred. Hence our poem.

In my general estimate of the poem I am in substantial agreement with the most recent and most thorough treatment it has received, that of Hugh Shields. [18] One very tempting suggestion by Shields needs to be examined. Remarking that if Jean d'Abundance was the author it is strange that no edition but that described by Du Verdier, which is no longer extant, appears to have been published at Lyon, whereas Picot lists one published at Rouen (*ca.* 1600), Shields notes that certain textual allusions seem to point to possible Norman composition: references to England in title and text and to English crowns; to the author's landing at Caux; perhaps also to the *Conards* of Rouen and to the towns of Louviers and Mantes. He also observes that Mlle. Droz casts implicit doubt on the accepted authorship in dating the *Recueil Trepperel,* of which this poem is No. 26, between 1502 and 1511, when Jean d'Abundance is unlikely to have been active. [19] But since Shields concludes that this dating is probably mistaken, and that the 1530's are the most likely date (as Picot had said), this last objection must be discarded.

If we had no information other than that provided by the extant copies of the poem, or even by all the references indepen-

---

of parody, Stylistic Parody and Exemplary Parody, a distinction that is clearly both valid and useful. As Professor Yunck remarks, Exemplary Parody was especially popular in the Middle Ages; and it is that variety that we find here.

[18] *Op. cit.,* pp. 112-116.
[19] *Ibid.,* p. 115.

dent of Du Verdier's, Shield's suggestion that a Norman wrote it would be almost too attractive to resist. I agree that there is a punning allusion to the towns of Louviers and Mantes (though I interpret it differently), and I feel even surer than does Shields that the reference to the *Conards* is to the organized society of Rouen (or Caen or Évreux). But I do not see how we can discard Du Verdier's testimony. When he says that his copy was printed at Lyon, without name or date, he surely knows whereof he speaks, for the description is circumstantial. We do not know his grounds for attributing the work to Jean d'Abundance, of course, and it is possible that he erred in this. But since we have no evidence to set against his statement, other than the fact that the author had some knowledge of Normandy, I think we must accept his attribution. The Rouen edition listed by Picot is hardly evidence, except of the poem's continuing popularity, for it is the *latest* printing before those of Silvestre and Shields.

We must therefore take the allusions to Normandy to be the natural consequence of the initial choice of locale — *Angleterre,* which I interpret as English Normandy, in view of the uniform reading of lines 17-18. I have no authority for supposing that *Angleterre* could still, in the 1530's, be a name applied to the Norman territory lost to England since 1450. But unless we transpose the two lines (cancelling the plural *-s* of *descendus*), as Shields suggests, there seems to be no other plausible interpretation. Whether the knowledge of Normandy is unusually precise for a court clerk of Pont St.-Esprit, I do not know; but my guess is that it is not. The strongest indication of special familiarity is the reference to the *Conards;* but this is exactly the sort of special information that a member of the *Bazoche* might be expected to possess, for the two organizations were fundamentally similar in purpose. All this of course leaves unanswered the question of why the original choice of locale fell on Normandy. In the present state of our knowledge, it is probably unanswerable.

One possible interpretation of all this evidence for the authorship and place and date of composition, however, would resolve the conflicts and doubts that I have listed, and would account for that initial choice of locale. That is that the poem as we have it is indeed the work of Jean d'Abundance, but that it is a *rifacimento* of an earlier poem, one composed before 1450, when the English lost Normandy: roughly a century earlier than any likely date of the reworking that we possess. Such an interpretation does not absolutely depend on a false identification by Mlle. Droz of the poem in the *Recueil Trepperel* with our version; but it would be interesting to examine that poem to see whether it lacks the positive later features: perhaps the reference to the Lombards and to Milanese groats, that to the *Conards*, and certainly that to English crowns of the rose, which led Shields to conclude that the printing must be later than the typygraphy had indicated to Mlle. Droz. For it strikes me that she might more easily have been wrong in identifying two texts with whose content she was not especially concerned than in dating the printing.

We should, by this interpretation, suppose that a *fatrasie* parodying the legend of the Fifteen Signs was composed, probably by a Norman, at an undetermined date before 1450 for an undetermined occasion — possibly for the *Fête des Fous*. This poem, with or without modification, would have been printed around 1502-1511, in the version of the *Recueil Trepperel;* and this form (or another) would have been reworked by Jean d'Abundance around 1536 as the *sermon joyeux* we have. I offer this hypothesis not as proved or even probably provable, but as one that allows for reference to Normandy as "Angleterre," to the *Conards,* to crowns of the rose, and to the Italian campaign of François I in this poem.

If No. 26 of the *Recueil Trepperel* should prove to be correctly identified with the poem of Jean d'Abundance, we must accept Shields' belief that Mlle. Droz erred in her dating. But the hypothesis here proposed would not have to be abandoned, since it does not depend upon the existence of that particular printed text. On the other hand, if that text does indeed differ in the ways that I have enumerated, it offers strong support to the hypothesis.

The later of our two little books survives in what may be a unique copy in the Bibliothèque nationale. The only notice of it that I have discovered is that of Shields, who describes it briefly and suggests that it may be relevant to the *sermon joyeux* of Jean d'Abundance. [20] Its title page reads as follows:

---

[20] *Ibid.,* p. 114.

"Les quinze Signes aduenuz és parties d'Occident, vers les Royaumes d'Escosse, & Angleterre, significatifz de la ruine, fin, & consommation du Monde. *Au peuple de France.* Par A. D. A Paris, pour Michel Buffet, demourant pres le College de Lysieux. AVEC PERMISSION. 1587."

This title suggests that of Jean d'Abundance strikingly, though the reference to the medieval legend is more specific than his. Yet, if it contains fifteen distinct signs, they are not clearly indicated, as those of d'Abundance are. Nor does the reference to the signs as appearing in the west and descending on England and Scotland suit the description very well. The title of the first section is "Des Signes merveilleux advenuz & descenduz és parties d'Escosse & Angleterre"; but neither Scotland nor England is mentioned in this section, and the only direction mentioned is the south. The second section, entitled "Signification des Signes prodigieux apparus sur plusieurs Regions des parties de l'Occident," is in prose, and it is more specific. But there the signs are seen in both the east and the west, though more violently in the west; and these meteorological displays, whatever they were, are said to have been seen running and rolling up to the borders of England.

I emphasize these discrepancies more than I should do if we were dealing with this text alone because of the possibility that the title was influenced by that of the earlier piece, that of Jean d'Abundance. The reference to fifteen signs would provide no special link, since this could equally well have been taken from almost any version of the medieval legend. But the resemblance of "aduenuz et descendus és parties d'Escosse & Angleterre" to "descendus du ciel au pais d'Angleterre" is quite special. [21] Whoever composed this title would appear to have done so with a view to seizing attention by identifying the book with as many popular compositions as possible. And since Picot lists three reprints of the monologue of Jean d'Abundance around 1540 and a fourth, in

---

[21] The resemblance of the titles only is in question, not that of the content of the two works, which is quite different, even to the referent of the word *Angleterre,* if I am correct in supposing that this, in the earlier work, means the parts of Normandy (and perhaps more) still held by Henry VI. The reference to Scotland is an addition in the later work: my discussion will suggest reasons for this.

Rouen, around 1600, its familiarity and continuing popularity are hardly contestable. But the later author had other concerns than drawing an easy laugh from the commonalty. Whatever the signs he offers, he is in dead earnest in presenting them as proofs that the days of Antichrist are at hand and in interpreting them as warnings against the manifest sins of the times, particularly that of Protestantism. The work is, in fact, a tract in support of the Catholic party in the wars of religion then racking France.

Formally, the work is curiously divided. Indeed, it is quite clear that it was conceived and written as three separate works, which have been joined to form a sort of preface (in couplets); an introduction (in prose, with occasional couplets or quatrains inserted — apparently quoted, though very likely from the author's own works); and a main text (in ten-line stanzas). In fact, the arrangement strikes me as so arbitrary that, though I do not doubt that "A. D." is the author of all three parts, I suspect that their present appearance in a single volume and under a common title is due to some other hand, most probably that of the publisher, Michel Buffet. If so, it was most likely this editor, too, who composed the title, if composition it may be called; for it is actually no more than a conflation of the titles of the three parts, with the addition of the word to specify *fifteen* signs, as though he recognized the author's echoing of d'Abundance's title (if my conjecture is correct) and wished to carry it a little farther. The most reasonable explanation of this rough-handed editorship is, as I shall try to show, that the author was dead before the book was published.

Physically, the book does not appear to have been composed and printed continuously by the same printer. Sheet A, which contains the prefatory poem and the first two pages of the prose tract, uses a large italic type, in which the poem is set except for its title and the last four lines, which are in roman. This same italic is used for the title and two quoted couplets in the prose, which is otherwise in the same roman. Sheet B, which continues the prose to the end and begins the final poem, uses what looks like the same roman for the prose but a smaller italic type for the verse, though two couplets inserted near the end of the prose are in the large italic of Sheet A. Sheet C, which begins with the last line of the fifth *dizaine*, returns to the large italic, switching to a roman smaller than that of A and B at C iii, which contains the last three *dizaines* and (again in the large italic, and on a separate page) the author's address to the reader.

It is possible that more than one printer was involved — one for Sheets A and C and another for Sheet B, perhaps. If this argues that Buffet was in a hurry to publish the book, the most obvious reason would be that the work was indeed recently written and that the events described were of a journalistic freshness. But this seems on the whole unlikely, nor does the bibliographical evidence strongly or clearly suggest it. It is hard to be certain just what the circumstances were.

The first part of this pamphlet, the poem in couplets, and the last of the large prose sections of the second part appear to describe some actual and recently observed meteorological phenomena, such as an unusual display of the aurora borealis; though, so far as I can see, the descriptions do not seem to be of the same events. But perhaps both are simply too fanciful to show a common factual basis that really existed. At any rate, they appear to describe something generally observed and discussed shortly before the two pieces were written. In this respect they call to mind one other literary allusion to the legend of the Fifteen Signs: that of *The Vision of Piers the Plowman,* where a notable storm is interpreted as one of the Signs of Doom. [22] Skeat identified the particular tempest to which Langland refers, and it is quite likely that somebody well enough qualified in this kind of historical research could identify the phenomena that "A. D." describes, thereby providing a quite accurate date of composition for the work. But my own admittedly amateurish efforts have not turned up any very promising identification.

The "signs" in the third, or stanzaic, section are mostly quite different from these natural phenomena and constitute a kind of Jeremiad on the evils of the times. It is true that an earthquake is listed among them and that this is one of the signs of nature actually found among those of the medieval legend of the Fifteen Signs, though there in more spectacular form. But most of the signs deal with the behavior of men, something very minor in the legend.

---

[22] See Heist, *The Fifteen Signs Before Doomsday,* pp. 189-190.

Apart from the legend, the occurrence of the plague, if plague it be, described in the tenth stanza might be identified historically. The outbreak should have occurred ten years before the date of the poem, but the place where it occurred is not specified. Plague seems to have been endemic in Paris for several years from about 1563-1564; and an epidemic in 1572 killed 50,000 in Lyon. But which, if either, of these outbreaks is referred to can hardly be determined from what the author says of it. His interest is political and moral, not scientific or historical, and details are vague. And since such is his bent, I take the famine of the following stanza to refer not to a particular serious crop failure, but to the rise of prices of agricultural produce in the latter half of the century, occasioned chiefly by higher farm wages. If that is what the author is writing about, it is unlikely that this detail will help us to date the composition of the work more closely than the date of publication does.

As I have already hinted, I have a candidate to propose as the author of these tracts. The book has never been listed among his works: partly, no doubt, because these works have never received a great deal of critical attention, but also because he has been presumed to have died eight years before Buffet published this one. But a number of reasons have led me to conclude with reasonable certainty that the author of this little book was a prolific and popular writer who produced some twenty known books in prose or verse between the years 1550 and 1578. His name was Artus Désiré.

As to the possibility of Désiré's being the author of this work, there is no real difficulty. He may indeed have been dead in 1587. But as I have already remarked, this would not have prevented somebody else —presumably the publisher— from printing any literary manuscripts that had survived their author. And the book has indeed the appearance of one scraped together from three originally separate compositions — each part has even retained its separate title in the printed form. Moreover, there is no obvious unlikelihood that Buffet should have had access to some of Désiré's papers after his death; for Buffet had in 1550 published Désiré's book *La Loyauté conscientieuse des Taverniers* (or *Ta-*

vernieres).[23] The presumption that Désiré was dead in 1587 is therefore of no importance to the question of his authorship of the present work, unless it can be shown that the writing also belongs to that approximate date. If so late a date of composition should be proved certain or likely, the date of Désiré's death does become important, of course. But the possibility of his being the author would still remain open, for the presumption of his prior death rests on a very shaky basis. It goes back to Niceron, who supposed that Désiré had died soon after 1578, since that was the date of his last identified work, *Le Retour de Guillot*. Of this Niceron remarks: "C'est un Dialogue entre *Guillot*, qui représente Desiré, & la Bergere. On y voit que Desiré etoit alors vieux & grison."[24] For lack of other evidence, this opinion has been accepted ever since, as by the Abbé Goujet[25] and Rigolet de Juvigny,[26] among those who have expressed any opinion. But a man may live on, old and gray, for a good many years after he calls himself so in verse, and this is no serious reason for supposing that Désiré's death was imminent in 1578.

If no chronological unlikelihood prevents us from accepting Artus Désiré as the author of this book, what reasons have we for believing that in fact he was so? To consider the most objective evidence first, there is the pseudonym *A. D.* given as the name of the author on the title page. I have consulted such dictionaries of pseudonyms as seemed relevant, but the only one that lists an "A. D." among sixteenth-century writers is J. M. Quérard, *Les Supercheries littéraires*.[27] And there Désiré is the only author listed as using this signature, as he does for his *Deffensoir de la foy chrestienne* (Paris, 1567).[28]

---

[23] See Rigoley de Juvigny, ed., *Les Bibliothèques françoises de la Croix du Maine et de Du Verdier, Sieur de Vauprivas*, I, 60.

[24] Jean-François Niceron, *Mémoires pour servir à l'histoire des hommes illustres dans la république des lettres. Avec un catalogue raisonné de leurs ouvrages*, Vol. XXXV (Paris, 1736), pp. 293-294.

[25] Claude-Pierre Goujet, *Bibliothèque françoise, ou Histoire littéraire françoise*, Vol. XIII (Paris, 1752), p. 132.

[26] *Les Bibliothèques françoises*, III, 169.

[27] Second ed., by Brunet and Jannet (Paris, 1869-1870), II, 32157.

[28] He also uses the inversion "Sutra Erised" as a pseudonym in *Les Regretz et complainctes de Passepartout et Bruitquicourt, etc.* (Paris, 1557), for what light that may throw upon his literary habits and turn of mind.

Further, though one can never hope to exclude all the men living in the decade or so that we are considering who *might* have written such a book, I have managed to identify only four known writers of this period with the initials *A. D.* They are Alphonse Delbene, who was Bishop of Albi in 1588; Artus Désiré; Antoine Du Verdier; and Antoine Dupinet. Of these, Dupinet may be excluded at once: he was a Protestant, and no Protestant can have written this strongly anti-Protestant book. Du Verdier is hardly more likely, for his tastes and style, as exhibited in his *Bibliothèque*, are quite incompatible with such a work as this. And Delbene, who was Abbé of Hautecombe in the year in which the book was published, is unlikely to have been rewarded the next year with a bishopric for such a production, however devoted it may be to the triumph of the Church over heresy. It is not a very episcopal performance.

The case is very different with Artus Désiré. For all his extant works characterize him as exactly the kind of earnest and eccentric enthusiast to have produced such effusions as the three parts of this book. He was at once an embarrassment and a possible tool for the secular and ecclesiastical rulers of France, and the second quality seems to have accounted for his survival, despite one desperately false step in the course of his ambiguous career. The 18th-century commentators could barely endure him. Niceron, the most severe, sums him up as follows:

Artus Désiré n'est connu que par un grand nombre [29] de mauvais Ouvrages, qui ne sont recherchés qu'à cause de leur rareté, & que par une action qui méritoit la corde.

On ignore de quel Pays il étoit, & l'on ne sçait le temps ni de sa naissance, ni de sa mort. Il est sûr seulement qu'il étoit Prêtre, & qu'il témoignoit de zele contre la Nouvelle Religion. Tous ses Ouvrages tendent à la combattre; mais comme la science & la capacité lui manquoient, il tâchoit d'y suppléer par des bouffonneries & des plaisanteries. [30]

---

[29] More than twenty, according to A. Delpy, *Essai d'une bibliographie spéciale*, I, 83; more than thirty, according to Georges Greute, ed., *Dictionnaire des lettres françaises* (Paris, 1951), I, 220.

[30] *Mémoires*, XXXV, 284.

Niceron continues with a sketch of what is known of Désiré's life, which consists chiefly of the act for which he deserved the rope. He was arrested in March, 1561, while bearing a request to Philip II of Spain to intervene in France to save the Catholic faith. For this crime he was sentenced to make an *amende honorable* and to be sequestered in a monastery, from which, however, he soon escaped. The Abbé Goujet tells us a little more concerning these latter circumstances:

Cette sentence fut éxécutée le 14 juillet de la même année [*sc.* 1561] quant à l'amende honorable. Mais la retraite du coupable chés les Chartreux ne fut pas longue. Soit qu'il n'y eût point d'ordre de veiller sur sa personne, soit qu'on ait voulu faciliter son évasion, il sortit assés promptement du couvent qui lui avoit été assigné, & dès 1568, il recommença à publier différens ouvrages à Paris, comme il avoit fait auparavant. [31]

Goujet also surmises that, though Niceron is correct in saying that we do not know his place of birth, Désiré was a Norman, "parce que son livre intitulé: *Les Combats du fidèle Papiste Pelerin Romain contre l'Apostat Antipapiste,* &c. on voit qu'il prend un intéret particulier à la Normandie, & qu'il ne fait mention d'aucun autre pays." [32]

And Goujet, though hardly ravished by the writing of Désiré, is considerably more tolerant of it than Niceron:

Je vous ai déja insinué que tous les ouvrages d'Artus Désiré tendent à combattre l'hérésie qui ne faisoit alors que trop de progrès en France. Mais outre qu'ils sont presque tous en vers, ou, si vous voulez, en prose rimée, genre d'écrire peu propre pour la controverse, on y voit en général plus de turlupinades que de raisonnements, plus d'injures que de preuves, plus de boufonneries que de sérieux & de gravité, plus de verbiage que de solidité. Et il y a lieu de croire que la nécessité, peutêtre encore plus que le zele, lui mit souvent la plume à la main. Je ne dirai pas cependant avec Pere Niceron, *qu'il manquoit de science & de capacité.* On voit par ses écrits qu'il avoit lû avec soin les livres saints, qu'il étoit au fait des points controversés, & qu'il n'ignoroit ni les objec-

---

[31] *Bibliothèque françoise,* XIII, 132.
[32] *Ibid.,* pp. 129-130.

tions des nouveaux hérétiques, ni les réponses peremptoires qui les renversent; mais il ne fit pas de ses connoissances l'usage reglé qu'il en devoit faire. Il donna aussi à la plus grande partie de ses écrits des titres bizarres, souvent ridicules, en quoi néantmoins il suivit autant le goût de son siècle que le sien propre. [33]

A silly century and a silly gentleman, from the point of view of the Age of Reason. But Goujet's view that Artus Désiré, if a fool, was not also an ignoramus seems juster than that of Niceron, who seems unable to overcome his outrage at Désiré's treason. No more can M. Rigoley de Juvigny, who cites M. de la Monnoye as his source, in a discussion of Désiré's name:

Quoiqu'on dise *Arturus* en Latin, on ne dit en François qu'Artus, & cet Auteur ne s'est jamais nommé autrement. Le Président de Thou, qui devoit naturellement, comme Béze, l'appeler en Latin *Artusius Desideratus*, l'appelle *Arturus Desiderius*. C'est ce fameux Artus Désiré qu'en 1561 le Prevôt des Maréchaux d'Orléans surprit chargé d'un paquet adressé à Philippe II, Roi d'Espagne, pour implorer son secours dans le besoin où se trouvoit la Religion Catholique en France d'avoir un protecteur également zélé & puissant. Artus, qui méritoit d'être pendu, en fut quitte pour faire amende honorable le 14 juillet de la même année, et de-là être conduit dans un Couvent de Chartreux où on l'enferma, mais d'où il se sauva quelque temps après, sans qu'il en fût autre chose. [34]

A list of the titles of the known works of Désiré that are preserved in the Bibliothèque nationale will give a sufficient taste of the extravagance to which Goujet objects and, I hope, also show why I think that both style and subject matter are the product of the same pen as the present work by "A. D." I take them from the catalogue of the library, with the brief bibliographical data there included; and I have listed them as nearly as possible in chronological order.

1. *Les Combatz du fidelle papiste, pélerin romain, contre l'apostat priapiste tirant à la synagogue de Genève, maison babilonicque des luthériens. Ensemble la description de la Cité de*

---

[33] *Ibid.*, pp. 132-133.
[34] *Les Bibliothèques françoises*, I, 60, n. 1.

Dieu assiégée des hérétiques. Rouen, 1550. 2 vols. in 1, 175 ff., fig. [35]

2. *Passevent parisien respondent à Pasquin rommain. De la vie de ceux qui sont allez demourer et se disent vivre selon la réformation de l'Évangile au païs jadis de Savoye, et maintenant soubz les Princes de Berne et seigneurs de Genève, faict en forme de dialogue.* N. p., 1556 (48 ff. 16°).

3. *Les Regretz et complainctes de Passepartout et Bruitquicourt, sur la mémoire renouvellée du trespas et bout de l'an, de feu très noble et vénérable personne maistre Françoys Picart, docteur en théologie et grand doyen de Sainct-Germain de l'Aucerroys.* Sutra Erised. Paris, 1557 (8°, Sig A—D).

4. *Les Articles du traicté de la paix entre Dieu et les hommes.* Paris, 1558 (Sig A—C).

5. *Les Disputes de Guillot le Porcher et de la bergère de S. Denis en France contre Jehan Calvin, prédicant de Genesve, sur la vérité de nostre saincte foy catholicque et religion chrestienne. Ensemble la Généalogie des hérét](_)cques et les fruictz qui proviennent d'iceulx.* Paris, 1559 (III—77 ff.).

6. *Les Batailles et victoires du chevalier céleste, contre le chevalier terrestre, l'un tirant à la maison de Dieu, et l'autre à la maison du prince du monde, chef de l'Église maligne. Avec le terrible et merveilleux assault donné contre la saincte cité de Jérusalem, figurée à nostre mère saincte Église, environée des ennemys de la foy.* Paris, 1560 (176 ff.).

7. *Plaisans et armonieux cantiques de dévotion, composez sur le chant des hymnes de nostre mère saincte Église à la louange de Dieu et de ses sainctz, qui est un second Contrepoison aux cinquante-deux chansons de Clément Marot.* Paris, 1561 (63 ff. 8°).

---

[35] Georges Greute, *op. cit.*, I, 220, remarks: "Certaines de ses oeuvres ont été éditées et illustrées à Rouen par des artistes de talent, les frères Dugort." Greute here states flatly that Désiré was born in Normandy and lived 1510-1579. Since he presents no evidence, it is unlikely that he has any beyond that which supports the conjectures of Goujet.

8. *Le Contrepoison des cinquante-deux chansons de Clément Marot, faulsement intitulées par luy "Psalmes de David", faict et composé de plusieurs bonnes doctrines et sentences préservatives d'hérésie.* Paris, 1562 (74 ff.) [36]

9. *Le Deffensaire de la foy chrestienne, avec le Miroir des francs taupins, autrement nommez luthériens.* Paris, 1567 (Sig A—K, woodcuts).

10. *Le Miroir des francs taupins, autrement dictz antechrists, auquel est contenu le deffensoire de la foy chrestienne.* Rouen, n. d. (Sig A—E). [37]

11. *L'Origine et source de tous les maux de ce monde, par l'incorrection des pères et mères envers leurs enfans et de l'inobédience d'iceux. Ensemble de la trop grande familiarité et liberté donnée aux servans et servantes, avec un petict discours de la visitation de Dieu envers son peuple chrestien, par affliction de guerre, peste et famine.* Paris, 1571 (50 ff.).

12. *La Singerie des Huguenots, marmots et guenons de la nouvelle derrision Théodobeszienne, contenant leur arrest et sentence par jugement de raison naturelle.* Paris, 1574 (8 ff. 8°).

13. *Les Grans abus et barbouilleries des taverniers et tavernières qui meslent et brouillent le vin. Avec la feinte réception et ruse des hostesses et chambrières enver leures hostes. Plus une réformation des taverniers et gourmandise.* Rouen, 1578 (93 pp. 12°).

14. *Le Ravage et déluge des chevaux de louage, contenant la fin et consummation de leur misérable vie. Avec le retour de Guillot le Porcher, sur les misères et calamitez de ce règne présent.* Paris, 1578 (55 ff. 8°).

It is obviously impossible here to characterize these works in detail. In general, Goujet's description of them is accurate. They are naïvely polemic, humorless in their humor, conservative to the

---

[36] Since the "Second Contrepoison" (see No. 7) had been published in the previous year, this is presumably not the first edition.
[37] Cf. No. 9.

point of reaction, but sincere almost to madness. The mind and method that produced them are those of the pamphleteer. Throughout Désiré's career all forms of Protestantism (the varieties of which he is not always careful to distinguish) were the chief targets of his attack, and his surviving works of the 50's and 60's of the century deal exclusively with these. In the early 60's he appears to have become aware of Marot's French versions of the Psalms [38] and devotes two books to rival sets of devotional lyrics, not neglecting to attack Marot at the same time.

In the 70's his cranky spleen is vented upon secular abuses, private and public: on the poor discipline of children and servants, in 1571; on the adulteration of wine and other sins of tavern-keepers, in 1578; and also in 1578, when he appears from his subjects to have done considerable traveling, on the wretched treatment of hired horses. At the same time, his attacks on heresy do not cease: *La Singerie des Huguenots* appeared in 1574; and *Le Retour de Guillot le Porcher*, with a character he had used in 1559 in a dialogue attacking Calvin, is published in the same volume as the polemic on the sad lives of livery horses in 1578, the year of his last positively identified publications.

But despite his fanatic eccentricity, and in the face of the 18th-century historians, his writing is technically competent enough for his modest aims. His matter may be foolish or dull, or both at once, but his rather glacial verse is an age away from the medieval jog trot of Jean d'Abundance. The classical verse of the Renaissance has transformed French versification, and Artus Désiré has learned to cope with its requirements, adequately if not brilliantly. The most obvious fault of his verse is one of which Goujet complains, that it is hardly suited to his matter, especially to the often vituperative style of controversy of the day.

Some faults of meter do indeed appear in the present verses, and in all three parts of the work. But since it is likely that the author did not oversee the publication of this book, we must

---

[38] Marot had published 30 of these as early as 1538. But since Désiré specifies 52, he apparently knew only the Geneva edition of 1543 — still nearly twenty years earlier, unless the missing first edition of Désiré's first *Contrepoison* was earlier than I have supposed: see note 36 above.

probably blame the printer for these blemishes. The second line
of the prefatory poem, for instance, has a syllable too many:

> France, ne doute pas que les Dieux au besoin,
> De tes affaires ont un trescharitable soin...

Presumably the author wrote either "ont un charitable" or "ont
trescharitable." But which? And in a couplet quoted in the prose
section (p. 50), what is the obviously omitted subject of *ont attaqué*,
which is needed both for sense and for meter?

> Vers l'Occident par grand desloyauté
> Ont attaqué la Royauté.

But there are very few such flaws, and I have attempted few
emendations beyond correcting a few misprints where the sense
makes the correct reading obvious. These misprints in themselves,
of course, confirm the view that the book was neither read in proof
by the author nor printed with extreme care, though I do not think
that they indicate unusual haste or carelessness, either. They are
normal printer's errors, and they speak neither for nor against the
authorship of Artus Désiré.

The two books here presented both stand, in their different
ways, outside the main intellectual currents that during the sixteenth century were transforming French culture. Among the
people whose opinions mattered, they had no future. Yet it would
be hard to say that, in the submerged nine-tenths of the French
cultural iceberg, they were either completely unimportant or even
remote from the center. The earlier, that of Jean d'Abundance, is
pure popular Late Medieval. The legend of the Fifteen Signs had,
on the serious theological level, long been rejected as unscriptural
and without authority, but it must have been apprehended by the
ordinary man as one of the teachings of the Church; for it was
regularly presented to him in that guise. It is now presented, in a
popular recitation, as a parody of that teaching. More sacred
matters were faring no better in the fifteenth and sixteenth cen-
turies. But this legend had no official support, and the weakening
of popular faith in it meant certain death for it in the near future.

That it had not quite died before the end of the century we know from other sources. And its continuing survival in popular tradition is made use of by Michel Buffet in 1587, when he supplies a title for the book that I attribute to Artus Désiré; for it must have been Buffet who supplied the word *quinze* in the title. I think Désiré, too, expects the ghost of the legend to stir in the memories of his readers, but this is less certain. For he does not, in any of the three titles of the individual parts of the work, or in the texts of these, speak of fifteen signs. He is too sound a theologian for that; and he may mean the recently observed phenomena that he seems to be describing to recall no more than the eschatological signs mentioned in Scripture.

Yet Désiré was certainly, like Buffet, well aware that the legend of the Fifteen Signs Before Doomsday had been in the mainstream of European consciousness from time immemorial. [39] If this legend —a part of the medievalism of Jean d'Abundance and a starting point for the religious polemic of Artus Désiré— was doomed along with that medievalism and that polemic, it still lived. And for an accurate understanding of the spirit of the sixteenth century, it is as important to note what was dying and the ways in which it was dying as to appreciate what was being brought to birth.

✿   ✿   ✿

The present edition of these two works requires some comment, particularly as regards that of Jean d'Abundance. Picot lists the following editions of the work, apparently all of which he had any knowledge or record. [40]

a. Les quinze grans & merveilleux signes ... Item plus la lettre descorniflerie ... & la chanson de la grande Gorre: le tout composé par maistre Tyburce ... Printed at Lyon, n. d. [*ca.* 1536].

This is the edition cited by Du Verdier and apparently not seen by any later bibliographer.

---

[39] In fact, for about 600 years, as my general study of the legend shows. Presumably these men of the sixteenth century would have assigned it an even longer history — one extending back to the time of St. Jerome, at least.

[40] *Romania*, XVI, 461-462.

b. Les quinze grans et merueilleux signes ... Item plus la lettre descorniflerie. No place or date [*ca.* 1540].

According to Picot, this is the edition cited by Brunet, *Manuel du libraire et de l'amateur de livres,* IV, col. 1029. Picot does not identify the edition of Brunet that he consulted. The fifth (Paris, 1863) describes this work in cols. 1030-1031 and lists two editions, of which the first seems to be Picot's *b,* though Brunet's title includes a word *(moult,* preceding *terrible)* that Picot omits. The second differs markedly from Picot's *b.* Brunet's notice is as follows: "Il se trouvait chez le duc de La Valliere (Catal. en 3 vol., n⁰ 2975, art 7) une édition de cette pièce, sous le titre suivant:

"Les QUIZE signes descendus en Angleterre. Auec la lettre descorniflerie, pet. in-8. goth. de 4 ff. Dans cette facétie la première pièce se compose de 140 vers de 8 syllabes, et la seconde est en prose. Cette dernière a été réimprimée récemment (voy Lettre de corniflerie)." [41]

The description of the duc de La Valliere's copy corresponds exactly to that of the text now bearing the number Ye 1327 in the Bibliothèque nationale, assuming that the Latin and pseudo-Latin at the beginning are counted as four lines. Since the number of lines, 140, could then be arrived at on the supposition that the second sign was omitted in the duc's copy, as it is in Ye 1327, we could feel certain that these two texts represent the same edition, and probably the same copy. But if these first four lines —which are printed as two and are only approximately describable as octosyllabics— were not counted in, the copy in the duc de La Valliere's library must have been one that included the four lines of the second sign.

c. Les quinze signes descendus en Angleterre. ⸿ auec la lettre descorniflerie. *Imprime nouuellement a Paris.* — ⸿ *Explicit.* Pet. in-8 goth. de 4 ff. Picot identifies this as the edition reprinted by Silvestre and describes a woodcut that follows the title.

---

[41] The reference to a reprint of *La Lettre descorniflerie* is to a lithographic facsimile published by Silvestre about 1832, and so before Silvestre had begun the *Collection* in which the present text (with another edition of *La Lettre*) occurs. See Brunet, III, col. 1024.

d. Les quīze signes ‖descendus en an‖gleterre. Auec la lettre descorniflerie. — *Finis.* S.l.n.d. [*v.* 1540], pet. in-8 goth. de 4 ff. de 27 lignes à la page, sign. A.

This edition has only a simple head title, reducing fol. 1, recto, to 18 lines of text. Picot's copy was numbered E. 472, c in the Bibliothèque municipale of Versailles (now Versailles munic. Goujet 164, according to Shields, who uses it for variant readings in his edition).

e. Les Quinze Signes descendus en Angleterre. Auec la lettre d'Escorniflerie. S.l.n.d. [Rouen, Nicolas Lescuyer, v. 1600], pet. in-8.

Picot's reference is to "Biblioth. de S. A. R. Mgr le duc d'Aumale (Cat. Cigongne, n⁰ 2096)."

f. Collection de Poésies, Romans, Chroniques, etc., publiée d'après d'anciens manuscrits et d'après des éditions des XVe et XVIe siècles. *Paris, chez Silvestre, [de l'imprimerie Crapelet],* 1838-1860. N° 25.

Silvestre's edition bears no date; but since it is the last number in that series, it was presumably published in 1860.

It would appear that Picot either used an edition of Brunet that did not mention the duc de La Valliere's copy of the poem or overlooked the reference. As I have remarked above, this copy seems to be identical with the text now in the Bibliothèque nationale. It is also very similar to Picot's *c;* but, lacking the specification *Imprime nouuellement a Paris,* it cannot be that one. And it is also very similar to Picot's *d,* and may in fact be identical with it if the four introductory lines were not counted by whoever prepared the description that Brunet quotes (see my discussion under *b,* p. 28 above).

We thus have three descriptions of texts —the Versailles copy, the Bibliothèque nationale copy, and the duc de La Valliere's copy— of which two may or may not be identical: the duc de La Valliere's and one of the others. Picot lists only the Versailles copy; so we must add either one or two more editions to his list. We must also add Shields' edition, published since the list was compiled, making a total of at least eight editions before the present one.

The Bibliothèque nationale copy, which constitutes the base of Shields' edition, is close to Picot's *b, c,* and *d,* and also to the La Valliere edition, if that is still another. It is perhaps especially close to *c,* and indeed, it appears to have issued from the same printing house; for it has, beneath the title, the same woodcut as that described by Picot as appearing in *c,* a very exact copy of which appears in Silvestre's reprint. The Bibliothèque nationale edition appears to have been prepared much less carefully than *c,* if Silvestre has represented the latter accurately, as he seems to have done. Not only have the four lines containing the second sign been dropped, but smaller differences throughout the poem give sense and meter inferior to those of *c.*

The form of the title of *e,* the latest edition before that of Silvestre, seems likewise similar to those we have been considering. On the basis of these descriptions, and especially of the forms of the titles, we may perhaps hazard a division of the editions into two major types, the Lyon type, consisting of *a* and apparently *b,* and a Paris type, comprising all the others. It is unfortunate that the Lyon type has not survived, since it was the oldest and the only one over which the poet may have exercised some control. Edition *b,* known only from Brunet's listing, may actually have been published in Paris, but its title resembles that of *a* so far as it goes. Its chief departures are that it contains only two of the three pieces in *a* and lacks the ascription to "Maître Tyburce." It is therefore apparently a transitional type and very likely the edition from which the Paris type is derived.

Since there seems to be no possibility of recovering the Lyon text, I have based the present edition on the one available that seems artistically superior, in what I take to be the spirit of Professor James Thorpe's recent exhortation to editors. [42] I have carefully compared the text of Silvestre's edition, which I use as my base, with photocopies of Bibl. nat. Ye 1327 and with the variants of this from the Versailles text that Shields lists, and I have noted all substantive differences, so far as I could judge that slippery matter.

---

[42] "The Æsthetics of Textual Criticism," *PMLA,* LXXX (1965), 465-482. It is now also the least accessible text, of course.

My treatment of the texts has been conservative. I have expanded the few abbreviations that occur, including the roman numerals *.v.* and *.viii.* in lines 45 and 65, respectively. [43] I have normalized *i, j* and *u, v* according to modern practice; and in general I have followed modern usage with capital letters (restricted to line-initials in the sources) and punctuation, including apostrophe, hyphen, and cedilla. Punctuation is almost absent in the sources, consisting of an occasional full stop (.) at the end of a section —the first follows line 5 and the second line 32, for instance— and a few diagonals (/), used to separate members of a series in the same line and for some other comma-like functions. I have not added accents, however, except for an acute on tonic *e* when final or followed by final *s*.

My treatment of the second text, that by "A. D.," is hardly editing at all, but more like simple transcription. I have expanded the rather frequent abbreviations (chiefly for nasals), and I have corrected several evident errors, as I have noted. Of the few emendations that I have attempted, most strike me as quite obvious. The arguable ones are those remarked in notes 4, 8, and 11. I have based these upon the demands of both the sense and the meter, and they are necessarily speculative.

I have modernized the use of *i, j* and *u, v*, on the assumption that *desja*, for example, is easily recognized as *déja*, but that *desia*, with its Italianate look, might cause a moment's hesitation. And I have partially modernized the punctuation, while preserving as much as possible of that which I found, and added or altered a few accent marks, where the text seemed to exhibit printer's oversights. But I have not thought it necessary or desirable to impose a whole modern system of accentuation or of punctuation upon this text.

I have thus not treated the two texts in quite parallel styles of editing, for they do not present exactly the same problems. The text of Jean d'Abundance comes to us with nothing that we can

---

[43] There is some question how these should be read: probably as ordinals, as I have done, but possibly as cardinals, as with *treize, quatorze,* and *quinze* (lines 100, 108, 116). Since there appears to be no fixed textual tradition of representing the numbers of these days, we must suppose that the spellings that occur represent printers' guesses.

recognize as a system of punctuation or accentuation; so I have supplied one, hoping to make the poem easier to read. But "A. D." 's work has its own systems, imperfectly applied; and so far as that of the accents is concerned, I have been content to regularize it on its own terms. I have tampered rather more with the punctuation, and I can hardly hope that I have always avoided inconsistency in superimposing a modern system upon it in some places and not in others. But a work of this sort I have preferred to touch with a light editorial hand. Reading the text, after all, presents few difficulties, and I hope that I have removed the worst of them without adding others.

Les Quinze Signes descendus en Angleterre [*]

In nomine patris prima
Et filii secunda,
Barbara potabaston,
Jamey regina celorum
5 De la et de ça. Amen, amen.
  Je suis venu par le moyen
Du roy Jesus en ceste terre,
Et suis descendu d'Angleterre,
Ou j'ay veu de grans merveilles.
10 Destouppez trestous voz oreilles,
Affin que puisses tous entendre,
Autant le grant comme le mendre,
Mes parolles, et retenir
Ce qui m'a fait icy venir:
15 Ne doubtez, c'est pour vostre bien.
En Angleterre, dont je vien,
Est advenu de tresgrans maulx
Descendus aux Pays de Caulx
Par la fortune du temps,

[*] Variants are from Bibliothèque nationale Ye 1327 (N) compared from a photocopy and Shields' edition, and from Versailles munic. Goujet 164 (V) as reported by Shields in his variant readings. I have assumed that it agrees with N where Shields does not specify a difference.

1-4 *Printed as 2 lines in all texts*
11 N Affin que me puissiez entendre; V que puissiez

20   Parquoy ont dit les anciens.
        Depuis que l'Entecrist fut né
        Il ne fut onc ung tel esté
        Si dangereux ne si perilleux.
        Quinze signes si merveilleux
25   Sont devallez: chascun en tremble.
        Ung chascun de vous se remembre
        De m'escouter ce que vueil dire.
            Le premier signe si n'est pas pire:
        Il gresilla feves nouvelles
30   Et pleut ung jour tables et scabelles,
        Des bancz, des selles, et chaslis,
        Et negea moutons et brebis.
            Le second signe, pleut gelines
        Et gresilla potz et chopines,
35   Mille yvrongnes criant la faim;
        Il pleut ung moys boteaux de foin.
            Le tiers signe fut autrement:
        Il pleut trois jours moulins a vent,
        Roues, rouelles, et chariotz,
40   Et negea huyt jours videcoqz.
            Le quart signe fut bien douloureux:
        Il pleut cinq jours vasches et beufz,
        Torteaux et amendes pelees,
        Et gresilla des poys pillez.
45   Le cinquiesme signe, il pleut enclumes,
        Barres de fer a grans escumes,

---

22 *N* Il ne fut ung autel esté; *V* veu ung tel
27 *N* De m'e. pour ouyr dire
28 *N, V* signe n'est pas le pire
30 *N, V* *omit second* et
31 *N, V* *omit* Des, des
33-36 *N* omits
35 *V* yvrongne
36 *V* trois moys
43 *N, V* pellee
46 *Silvestre* grant

Beurre frais et haren sallé,
Et pleut deux mil septiers de blé.
Le sixiesme est bien certain:
50 Il pleut poysles et potz d'arain,
Andouilles, saulcisse, et boudins,
Et negea lievres et connins.
Des Lombards il plut une undee
Qui ont houlcé noz cheminees
55 Depuis le hault jusques au bas;
Les Françoys leur ont fait leur cas.
Le septiesme signe, au matin,
Il plut le jour poinssons de vin,
Depuis le matin jusque a vespres,
60 Et vers le soir il plut des prestres,
Qui nous ont fait beaucoup de peine:
La ville en estoit toute plaine;
Ilz boivent bien quant il fait trouble
Demyon de vin pour ung double.
65 Le huytiesme signe, c'est chose vraye,
Il pleut de belles robes de soye,
Veloux, satin, et cramoysi,
Et puis negea du laict boully,
Formage mol, et cresmes doulces;
70 Il gresilla coupeurs de bources:
De vous garder ayez memoire,
Tant au marché comme a la foire.
Le neufviesme signe, il pleut aprés
Brigandines et blancz harnois,
75 Voulges, picques, et hommes d'armes,

---

48 *N* sextiers
49 *N, V* Le .vi. signe est
50 *V* d'estain
53 *V* De *for* Des
59 *V* au *for* a
66 *N* des belles; *V* de belle robe
72 *N, V omit* Tant
75 *V* Douges *for* Voulges

Et negea Jacopins et Carmes,
Merceries, peignes, esguillettes.
En aprés il pleut des fillettes;
De cela je n'en doubte rien—
80   Je croy, moy, que tout viendra bien.
    Le dixieme signe pour abreger,
Il pleut des joueurs de bouclier,
Fers a charrue, et corne de vache,
Plus d'ung cent de sergens a masse,
85   Baillifz, vicontes, et lieuxtenans,
Qui survindrent tous pour ung vent.
Toutes les villes en sont fournies;
Jamais on ne vit telles pluyes.
    Le unziesme signe fut aventures:
90   Il plut abbayes et masures,
Moines noirs, nonnains, Celestins,
Chartreux, Cordeliers, Augustins,
Gens aspres assez, je vous asseure:
C'est une bonne nourriture.
95   Et puis aprés il gresilla
En latin, "Ego flagella."
    Le douziesme fut autre chose:
Il plut des escus a la rose,
Des rides prou, et des ducatz.
100   Il plut ung moys des advocatz,
Des notaires, et des procureurs:
Jamais ne furent si eureux—
Ce fut au monde ung beau tresor—
Et gresilla lunettes d'or.

---

83 *V* cornes
86 *N* vindrent; *V* viendront
87 *N, V omit* les
92 *N, V* Chartreurs
93 *N, V* apres
96 *N* ergo
97 *N* Le .xii. signe fut autre; *V* fut ung autre: *both omit* chose
99 *N, V omit* prou

105   Le treize signe n'est pas let:
      Il plut des gens du monde helet,
      Chanoynes, et quoqueluchez,
      Conars, martins, mariez:
      De cela fut chiere ouverte;

110   Ce fut au pays une grant perte
      Que celluy qui les fist porter
      En doint le pays delivrer.
         Le quatorze signe, sans doubtance,
      Il pleut des loups telle abondance

115   Que, entre Louviers et Mante,
      On en eut bien finé soixante;
      Et aprés il plut des saulmons
      Et gresilla tant de chappons,
      De faisans, et de videcoqz,

120   Flesches de lard a grans minotz.
         Le quinze signe et le derrain,
      Il plut ung jour quartiers de pain,
      Que onc de l'estraine bribiers
      Ne furent jamais aussi fiers,

125   Et ne feront que requerir
      Dieu, que luy plust les maintenir
      Ainsi tout le temps de leur vie,
      Et de faire tousjours tel pluye.
         Aprés il pleut jattes, corbeilles,

---

106   *N, V* mont; *V* de *for* du
108   *Silvestre* marmetins
111   *N, V* pleuver
115   *V* louvriers amente
120   *N* mulotz
122   *N* .xv. jours
125   *N, V* faisoyent
126   *All texts have* qui *for* que; *Shields prints* qu'i, *perhaps correctly*
127   *N, V omit* Ainsi
128   *N* autel; *V* telle

130 Vaisseaulx, barilz, plaines bouteilles,
    Gros de Millan en gybecieres,
    Et negea bateaulx és rivieres.
    Et quant ce vint aprés-midy,
    Il plut du formage rosty,
135 Aulx, ongnons, poires, et pommes,
    Tant de femmes et aussi d'hommes,
    Et aussi plusieurs gens de guerre,
    Assez pour le pays conquerre
    Du grant royaume de Turquise,
140 Et de toute la terre de Venise.
    Ainsi signé je ne scay quant—
    Et pource passez vous a tant—
    Par ung marchant qui tousjours mocque,
    Que on appelle Halessenocque.

       Finis.

---

130 *N* baritz
132 *N, V* et rivieres
134 *V* Il plu fromages et rosty
136 *N* et de hommes
139 *N* Turquie
140 *N, V* Et toute la
142 *V* assez *for* passez
144 *N* appelloit

EXPLANATORY NOTES

Line 3. Shields, who notes Picot's evidence that the first four
lines were part of the common property of the authors
of farces, suggests a possible indecent suggestion in *Pota
baston,* comparing the Italian "per la potta della virgine!"

4. In his quotation from V Picot prints this as *J'ayme* — a poor
reading, I think, even though I cannot explain *Jamey.* If
this were the French *j'aime,* we should expect *reginam.*
Shields prints *J'amey,* which is open to the same objection.

17-18. Shields suggests reversing the order of these lines and
emending to *descendu* 'landed' to agree with *je.* All the
texts have the present reading, however, and I have sug-
gested interpreting *Angleterre* to mean most of Normandy
(see pp. 13-14 above). The positive references to *Conards,*
Louviers, Mantes, and *Coqueluchiers* seem certainly to
place the events in Normandy, though they are said
to occur in *Angleterre.* Note too that Mantes was in
Normandy at the time of the English occupation, though
returned to the crown in 1453.

30. *Scabelles:* 'stools' — modern *escabeaux.*

36. *Boteaux:* 'bundles' — diminutive of *botte.*

40. *Videcoqz:* usually 'woodcocks,' as in l. 119; here also?

44. Shields suggests that *poys pillez* involves a pun: 'ground
peas' or 'farces, *sotties.*'

46. Godefroy gives *écumoire* 'skimmer' as one meaning of *es-
cume* in OF; but this sense does not seem right here,
unless we emend *a* to *et,* as perhaps we should. Could it
be the still current sense of 'slag, dross,' used in smelting?
Shields makes nearly the same point.

48. *Septiers:* N's *sextiers* is historically correct. The *p* represents a reverse spelling, the pronunciation of the first syllable having become identical with that of *sept.*

53-56. See p. 10 above.

63-64. Shields suggests an equivocation on *vin trouble.* A demion is a *demi-chopine* or half-pint. Shields explains *double* as a small coin worth two *deniers;* but is it perhaps a variant of *doublier,* a two-pint container?

74. *Brigandines:* corselets of iron plates riveted on leather, which replaced the hauberk.

86. Shields suggests that *pour ung vent* may mean 'on the least excuse.'

93. Shields prints *aprés* for *aspres;* it is rather modern *âpres* (pl.) 'sharp-set.'

96. *Ego flagella:* 'I am the whip,' with the Latin neut. pl. taken as fem. sg.

98. Shields (p. 115) notes that the earliest extant English crowns of the rose, first decreed in 1526, are of the mid-thirties. This is an important —indeed crucial— point in confirming Picot's dating of the poem.

99. *Rides* (a variant of *ridres*) were coins worth fifty sous. *Prou* (modern *preux*) has the sense of 'enough, many,' as in *Peu ou prou.*

106. Shields prints *mont Helet* but understands it no more than I. If *mont* is correct, as the meter suggests, apparently the printer of Silvestre's original did not understand it, either. Du Cange, *s. v. Abbas Conardorum,* illustrates his entry with a reference to a book published at Rouen in 1587. After giving the title (amounting to an outline of the contents), he adds: "Eodem in Libello occurrunt Litteræ patentes Abbatis *Conardorum,* quibus ad Cardinalatum quemdam evehit nomine De Montalinos." As a very long shot, one might conceive that there has been both garbling and misunderstanding here, and that the mock cardinalate was to be occupied not by somebody so named but by someone of the people of Mont (H)al- plus a possible suffix, perhaps *-et,* dropped in forming the derivative in *-inus.* This also involves the assumption

either that *de* might occur with the accusative or that
the printer misset it for *-is*. Obviously I have small confi-
dence in this suggestion. On the other hand, De Montalinos seems an unlikely Norman name.

107.   *Quoqueluchez,* more usually *coqueluchez:* evidently 'wearing
a *coqueluche,* or hood.' But this should probably be read
as *coqueluchiers,* pl. of a noun, wich Godefroy defines as
one "qui porte un coqueluchon," as Shields suggests.
Godefroy illustrates with the quotation "Comme Conards,
coqueluchiers (Ch. de L. XII instituant la Bazoche, citée
dans un ârret du parlem. de Rouen du 17 déc. 1711)."
Godefroy does not list *Conards,* about which group there
is a good deal in Du Cange, who describes their organiza-
tion and activities. He says that in Rouen they were suc-
cessors to the *Coqueluchiers* and dates their foundation
from the time of Marot. Both *Conards* and *Coqueluchiers*
seem to have been fraternal groups organized on mock-
clerical lines, with public amusement and satire their
main purpose, somewhat like the *Bazoche.* Cf. the still
active *Blancs Moussis* of Stavelot, who also claim a 16th-
century origin.

108.   *Conars, martins, mariez:* for the *Conards,* or *Cornards,* see
the preceding note. I have found no reference to *marmetins,* as Silvestre prints the word, and the reading *martins*
seems more plausible. Huguet lists "*Faire le diable sainct
Martin* — Se démener" and notes that the devil is called
"l'estaffier de saint Martin," citing Rabelais, IV, 23. Cf.
also *martiner* 'drink to excess,' which Huguet cites, quot-
ing Rabelais, II, 28: "Un chascun de l'armée commencza
martiner, chopiner, et tringuer de mesmes." I therefore
suggest that *martin* means something like 'reveler.' *Mariez*
seems most likely to exhibit a sense of *marier* in the argot
listed by Huguet: "(En argot). *Marier.* Pendre.—*Anguée,*
c'est-à-dire pendu: si aucun de leurs compagnons a esté
angué, ils diront: *Il a esté marié.*" If this is the derivation
here, we must suppose an extension of the sense from
'hanged' to 'gallowsbird.'

109. *Chiere ouverte:* the sense 'welcome' familiar in OF and ME
seems adequate.

115. *Louvier* seems to have one of the senses that Huguet lists
for *louviere,* 'wolfskin coat *(casaque).*' A *mante* is a cloak,
not always of wolfskin, of course. The sentence is also to
be taken as meaning 'between Louviers and Mantes,' two
towns of medieval Normandy, as Shields says. But I doubt
that the pun is on 'wolf-hunters and tall stories,' as he suggests. The coincidence of these two towns lying relatively
close together and both bearing the names of outer
garments had doubtless provoked a familiar jest, here
repeated. To cite a recent parallel, the late Father Paul
Grosjean once told me of a comic question-and-answer
dialogue familiar when the main Brussels-Ghent railway
line ran through the neighboring towns of Lede and
Schellebelle: "Schellebelle?" "Lede." The pun is on
"Est-ce qu'elle est belle?" "Laide."

120. Shields explains the *mulotz* of N as 'mules,' 'haystacks,'
or 'fieldmice.' But V has *minos,* agreeing with Silvestre's
minotz. A *minot* is a measure (half a *mine* or a quarter
setier).

131. Shields translates "Milanese groats in purses," noting that
Louis XII minted groats at Milan in 1499 and that at
least as early as 1556 an inn at Évreux bore the sign "le
gros de Mylan." As he says, this is probably a coincidence.

Les quinze Signes ad-
uenuz és parties d'Occident, vers
les Royaumes d'Escosse, & Angleterre, significatifz de la ruine,
fin, & consommation du Monde.

Au peuple de France.

Par A. D.

A PARIS

Pour Michel Buffet, demourant pres le College

AVEC PERMISSION

1587

DES SIGNES MERVEILLEUX ADVENUZ & DESCENDUS ÉS PARTIES
D'ESCOSSE & ANGLETERRE. *

France, ne doute pas que les Dieux, au besoin,
De tes affaires ont un trescharitable soin;
Voicy qu'avant le temps, des maux qui t'environnent,
Pour t'y faire pourvoir, les signes ils te donnent.
C'est que Cynthie, estant en extreme decours,
Et sous nostre Orizon Phebus tenoient leurs cours,
Pour oster l'argument aux discoureurs de dire
Que ce fussent vapeurs que l'un ou l'autre attire,
Qui font à nostre veue estrange impression,
Sans en attribuer à Dieu l'intention.

Ce jour d'aspect sextille tetrique Saturne
De rayons tenebreux le Soleil importune,
Qui nous vient preparer & desja concevoir
Des Cometes qu'il forge à bien tost faire voir.
Le Ciel lors sa couleur toute bleue a rendue
Du costé de Midy en fort longue estendue,
Parmy la grand clarté des astres, qui par fois
Eslançoient leurs rayons en mil & mil endroicts.
Puis, soudain, au milieu de l'azuré nuage
L'air en blancheur s'est veu enfler comme, en naufrage,
Sont les voyles bouffans du vent impetueux.
Un voyle blanc à l'un se represente aux yeux,
Et l'autre estime plus qu'en estendart se forme,
Comme d'autre costé voye de laict a forme,

* The readings here given are those of Buffet's edition, Bibl. nat. D 49478.

L'an que Juno, Mercure allaictant espandit
Parmy le Ciel auquel un blanc cercle rendit.
Mais quand cest estendart par ses replis undoye,
Des astres à l'entour, il semble faire voye [1]
À gros brandons de feu au concave allumez,
Courans deçà, delà, comme estans animez,
L'un à l'encontre l'autre, où l'on voyoit les armes
Que noz plus vieilz Gaulois portoient en leurs allarmes:
Gros dards ou javelots passer se fracassans,
L'un l'autre au rencontrer, les nues s'esclattans
Aux coups qu'entre-donner les lances paroissoient,
Dont les esclats ardans par le vague air voloient.
Peu à peu l'estendart tandis s'esvanouyt,
Puis de rechef revint, mais gueres ne se vit. [2]
Ainsi du Toutpuissant la faveur debonnaire,
Lassus à poinct nommé, ces signes fit pourtraire
À ces preux Chevaliers, sur Paris mesmement,
Comme à l'ordre & au lieu qui principalement
Servent de seur appuy, par lequel la couronne
Retient sa Majesté en ce Lys qui fleuronne.
Arborez l'estendart, Chevaliers valeureux;
De sa pure blancheur soyez tant desireux
Que pas un seul de vous de son ombre s'absente,
Puis que le Ciel benin d'en haut le vous presente.
Afin que toy, o France exposee au malheur,
De te voir desmembrer par discorde & fureur,
De deux camps fraternelz, tu puisses recongnoistre
De quel party Dieu veut ton repos se mettre.
Le droict chemin qu'on tiendra sans feintise,
Pour tout [3] salut, est de suyvre l'Eglise.
Et du vray but qu'on tiendra le plus seur,
C'est [4] ne manquer à son predecesseur.

A Dieu soit gloire.

---

[1] voir.
[2] veid.
[3] tous.
[4] Gist. *This seems to require a preposition* (en *or* à) *for the sense 'consists in'; and adding one would spoil the meter.*

Signification des Signes prodigieux apparus sur plusieurs Regions des parties de l'Occident.

Il est certain qu'entre toutes choses qui se presentent à la veue des hommes, n'y a rien en ce monde qui plus nous donne à penser, voire qui plus nous esbranle par craincte, esperance, espouventement & admiration, que les merveilles prodigieuses, que Dieu selon ses jugemens secretz & incomprehensibles nous faict voir tant en la terre qu'au Ciel. Entre lesquelz ceux des Cieux sont plus considerables, pour autant que Dieu qui y habite comme en son propre domicile, lors qu'il nous faict descouvrir en iceux contre tout ordre de nature, quelque apparition miraculeuse, ou vision prodigieuse: comme de Comettes en façon de glaives, de feu, claires, tenebreuses, chevelues, barbues, torches, flambeaux, colonnes, Dragons, multiplicité de Lune ou de Soleil, eclipse d'iceux, armees & combatz divers, tant de cavallerie que d'infanterie, mesmes par les Demons, pluyes de sang, de terre, de pierre, de fer, de divers animaux, sans parler des gresles, foudres & tonnerres extraordinaires & espouventables: certainement, c'est lors que Dieu nous veut advertir, faisant de telz prodiges ses postes & Heraux, ainsi que parle David.

> *Des vens aussi diligens & legers,*
> *Faict ses Heraux, postes & messagers,*
> *Et foudre & feu fort prompts à son service,*
> *Sont les sergens de sa haulte justice.*

C'est lors, di-je, que Dieu desirant que nous rentrions en nous-mesmes, voyant nostre desesperee obstination, nous envoye comme pour avant-coureurs de sa Justice, plusieurs merveilleuses impressions en l'air, nous menassant pour le nombre infiny de noz offences, & nous advertissant, afin que corrigions noz moeurs pervers, & vices desbordez, ainsi que dict le poete.

> *Pense-tu que Jupin sa vengeance ayt laissee,*
> *Quand sur un arbre hault sa foudre il a lancee?*

De ces apparitions ont amplement escrit sainct Augustin, Eusebe, Josephe, Titelive, Julius obsequens, Plutarque, Valere, & autres

infinis autheurs, & plusieurs modernes, sur ce qui s'est presenté
de leur temps. Et sans m'amuser à esplucher les causes, naissances
& origines de telles apparitions, deffigurans horriblement la face
du Ciel, qui nous doit plustost donner tesmoignage de la gloire de
Dieu. Seulement j'adjousteray que telz divins messages nous doivent servir en particulier pour nous abbaisser & humilier envers
Dieu, par prieres, jeusnes & aumosnes, afin de prevenir par bonne
repentance la fureur divine, qu'elle ne s'embraze contre noz deme-
rites & que nous apprehendions les jugemens de Dieu. Et en
general que nous deplorions la calamité du temps present, & sup-
plions la majesté divine qu'il luy plaise regarder de son oeil
pitoyable la pauvre & desolee France, par le moyen de quelque
salutaire concorde.

Parce que ordinairement telles impressions, caracteres, figures
& combatz qui se font au Ciel, viennent à presager quelques sig-
nalees revolutions, mort de grands Seigneurs, mortalité de peuple,
batailles & guerres sanglantes, incursions d'estrangers, ruine de
plusieurs Citez, & autres piteux evenemens. Non que je vueille
adjouster foy aux resveries des Astrologues judiciaires, ains seulement par les infiniz anciens & modernes examples advertir un
chacun de faire son devoir pour impetrer de Dieu pardon & mercy.

> *Vers l'Occident par grand desloyauté*
> *Ont attaqué la Royauté.*

> *Et Dieu a dict: vous aurez Roys & Princes,*
> *À mon adveu dompteront voz Provinces.*

Et afin qu'il ne semble que les advertissemens cy dessus soient
en vain publiez, il a esté notoirement veu en la France plusieurs
signes merveilleux au Ciel de nuées tresobscures en forme de
forest, les unes venant de la partie d'Orient, avec celles de l'Occident significatives de tresgrande violence. Et combien que le
vent vint d'Orient, si est-ce que celles d'Occident venoient de plus
grande impetuosité, & aux rencontres s'eslevoient en la partie de
Septentrion du bas en hault, à plusieurs fois & divers endroicts
des clartez estroictes & longues, donnant tresgrande splendeur,
puis de fois à autre n'apparoissoit aucune lueur, jusques à ce que
nouvelles clartez treslongues & peu larges, avec autres obscuritez

de pareille longueur & largeur, les unes d'Orient, les autres d'Occident, de rechef se venoient aheurter, dont de bas en hault s'eslevoient pareilles clartez que celles desquelles avons ja parlé, comme flamme d'artillerie, & girandolles arificielles, montans en forme de fuzées en l'air, puis descendans en pluye dorée, et dont se discernoit aysément la fumée, & encores darder ardeurs & pouldres, en triangle de la partie [5] de Midy, courans & roulans jusques aux extremitez du pays d'Angleterre, qui dura jusques sur le minuict, la veille du jour sainct Michel, avec signes de grande frayeur, & Comettes fort lucides esdictes parties opposites. Ce que ces Signes ainsi divisez & entrelassez peuvent certainement signifier [sont] les divisions qui se publient en mainctes Regions & contrees des religions contraires les unes autres, & de plusieurs sortes; lesquelles causent aux circonvoisins d'icelles les uns devenir ennemis contre leurs grands amis, lesquelz par ce moyen, cherchent d'abastardir l'excellence & domination des plus grandz Roys & Princes que Dieu par sa beneficence a sur nous establiz, pour le reiglement de tenir en estat tous peuples & nations en son obeissance, & nous manifester sa justice, pour pouvoir parvenir apres ceste vie à la felicité.

On pourroit demander d'où procederoit la ruine des Regions d'une grande partie d'Allemaigne, en laquelle peu à peu le grand Turc s'advance & usurpe ce qu'il peut.

> *Et aussi des Anglois leur mortelle ruine,*
> *C'est qu'ilz ne font estat ny de Roy, ny de Royne.*
> *Ilz veulent seulement eux-mesmes maistriser,*
> *Et user de Justice qu'ilz ne peuvent priser.*

En effect telles nations de gens se contentent plus d'estre domptez par un infidelle, que de leur propre & naturel Seigneur, qui par droicte, equité & justice repousseroit l'ambition & convoitise de telz pernicieux, si à leur souverain portoient obeissance.

> *Pour s'estre mescogneuz en Flandre de leur Roy,*
> *Et desvoyez de premiere croyance,*
> *Sont maintenant en piteux desarroy,*
> *Et en peril de tresgrande souffrance.*

---

[5] parrie.

Des Signes merveilleux & terribles, significatifz de la ruine,
fin, & consommation du monde.

Consideré les grans maux qui se font
Contre l'honneur du sauveur venerable,
Esbahy suis que la terre ne fond
Dessoubs les piedz du peuple miserable.
Depuis que Dieu crea l'homme muable,
Il ne courut tant de sedition,
De tromperie, & cavillation,
Qui faict ce jour par la machine ronde:
Dont croire faut sans dubitation,
Que sommes pres de la fin de ce monde.

Prouver je veux par les lettres divines
Aux gens remplis de folastre argument,
Que ce jourd'uy nous voyons tous les signes,
Qui sont predits du signal jugement.
Pource Chrestiens de bas entendement,
Qui cognoissez que Dieu est irrité:
Recognoissez vostre infidelité,
Qui vous prepare une aspre recompense:
Amendés vous, car pour la verité
La fin du monde est plus pres qu'on ne pense.

Au grand salut de nous tous & des nostres
Il est escrit en monsieur saint Mathieu,
Qu'un certain jour les glorieux Apostres
Benignement demanderent à Dieu,
Quel [6] signe aurons en ce terestre lieu
Pour le tesmoing de son advenement,
Quand il viendra tenir son parlement
Que tout sera purgé du feu divin:
Lors il leur dit tresfamilierement
Ce qui [7] s'ensuit denotant nostre fin.

---

[6] Qu'el.
[7] qu'il.

Gardés (dit-il) que ne soyez seduicts:
Car plusieurs gens de damnable renom
En ce temps la seront si mal induicts,
Qu'ilz corrompront tout mon divin Canon:
Furtivement ilz viendront en mon nom
Preschant erreurs à haute voix & cris,
Et se diront estre les propres Christs
En declarant l'evangile au rebours:
Dont nous apert par ces sainct mots escrips
Que sommes pres de la fin de noz jours.

Or, je vous prie, arrestons nous icy
En penetrant le texte evangelique,
Et regardons si le temps n'est ainsi
Que nous predit Jesus Christ Deifique:
Voyons nous pas en ce regne impudique
Les susdits Christs au monde orbiculaire
Qui vont troublant le pauvre populaire?
Ouy, vrayment (ce qu'on n'a point amors),
Signefiant que Dieu en sa colere
Viendra de brief juger les vifs & mors.

Les Libertins aveuglés & deceuz
Qui ont trouvé l'eloquence imparfaicte,
Me pourroient tous alleger cy dessus,
Qu'ilz ne sont pas les premiers de leur secte,
Et que leur loy miserable & infecte
Ne vient point d'eux, mais d'autres gens de bien,
Comme de Hus, qui ne valut onc rien,
De Depraga, & d'autre Vviclevistes,
Cousins germains du maudit Arrien
Qui fut long temps devant les Lutheristes.

Quant à ce poinct, je dy pour repliquer
Qu'ilz sont au vray les premiers inventeurs
De dire Christ sans Jesus invoquer,
Et ceux que Dieu a reprouvez menteurs:
C'est à sçavoir, les faux predicateurs

Qui sus la fin se doivent eslever,
Dont ilz feront plusieurs peuples resver,
Et abusez par ce predict mot 'Christ';
Par quoy chacun peut juger & prouver
Que precurseurs ilz sont de l'Antechrist.

En outre plus, l'eternel Dieu nous dict
Qu'aux derniers jours le peuple mecanique
S'eslevera par un faux contredict,
L'un contre l'autre, à l'espee & à picque,
Gent contre gent, malheureuse & rustique,
Lors s'armera de haubert et de heaume, [8]
Et le royaume contre le royaume
S'eslevera en debatz & contens,
Il n'y a donc Evangile ne Pseaume
Qui ne predise estre à la fin du temps.

Voyons, Chrestiens, voyons si ce jourd'huy
Gens contre gens n'ont pas grand impropere:
Où est vertu? helas, où est celuy
Qui à present en ce monde prospere?
Avez vous veu le filz contre le père,
Et le voisin encontre le voisin,
Battre, frapper, si que le Sarrasin
A plus de foy en sa loy Sarrasine
Que le Chrestien n'a au frere ou cousin,
Et le cousin à sa propre cousine?

Or puis dix ans quelle peste terrible
A il couru par les villes & bourgs;
N'a on pas veu un danger si horrible
Qu'on delaissoit les citez & faulxbourgs?
N'a on pas veu si merveilleux decours
De maladie aspre & contagieuse,
Que pour fuyr [9] mort pestilencieuse

---

[8] de haubert le heaume.
[9] suyr.

Le pere & mere abandonnoient l'enfant,
Nous demonstrant que l'ame bien heureuse
S'approche fort du regne triomphant?

O, bon Chrestien, en ton esprit rumine
Ces signes grands que tu vois devant toy;
Ne vois tu pas en France la famine
Quoy qu'abondance y soit, dont en esmoy
Je suis, aussi que pour or ny aloy,
Ne pour parens, ou grands amis acquis,
Les vivres y sont si treschers & requis,
Qu'à bien grand' peine trouver blé en nul lieu? —
Nous denotant par ce grand signe exquis
Qu'en bref aurons le jugement de Dieu.

La terre aussi, n'a elle pas tremblé
En aucuns lieux impetueusement,
Et le Soleil de tenebres comblé
Perdu clarté, en son haut element?
Si a pour vray, qui est commencement
De desplaisir & tribulation,
Et que Dieu veut par disposition
De droict divin visiter son Eglise,
Où il fera grosse punition
Le jour yreux de sa crainctive assise.

S'ensuyt encor autre Signe evident
Que Dieu nous baille en sa saincte escriture:
Il nous predict comme grand president
Du temps crainctif toute nostre adventure.
Les gens, dict-il, de mauvaise nature
N'auront en eux aucune charité,
Et pour raison, si grande iniquité
Abondera entre les faux confreres,
Qu'il n'y aura nulle fidelité,
Ne nulle amour entre voisins & freres.

Or sommes nous maintenant en ce temps,
Homme n'y a qui le puisse nier:

Car nous voyons tous les Signes patens
Qui doivent estre en ce regne dernier.
Nous voyons Dieu & ses sainctz renier,
En blasphemant sa divine puissance,
Qui donne à tous certaine congnoissance
Que l'Antechrist, filz de perdition,
Est sur le poinct de prendre sa naissance
Pour commencer sa predication.

Or donc, humains qui oyez & voyez
L'iniquité qui sur la terre abonde,
Tant que pourrez fuyez ces dévoyez,
Qui par les champs vont seduire le monde:
Le faux serpent tentateur & immonde
Vous poursuyt fort pour vous faire lascher
La saincte hostie, où gist la digne chair
De Jesus Christ, redempteur pitoyable.
Pource gardez d'en ces lacqz trebucher
Et de doubter au sacrement notable.

Ne sont ce pas grandz signes apparens
De ces cas là que voyons vous & moy?
Quelle [10] amytié y a il aux parens,
Et où sont ceux qui observent la loy?
Bref, à present l'home n'ayme que soy,
Et son amour est si particuliere
Qu'à son prochain elle n'est familiere,
Sur quoy pouvons dire & conjecturer,
Que le monde est à la saison derniere
Qui ne peut plus guere de temps durer.

Voyons nous pas tous ces merveilleux signes
Que nous rescript le dessusdit sainct Paul?
Voyons nous pas les personnes malignes
Qui laissent Dieu pour croire à l'esprit fol?
Voyons nous pas les hommes plein de dol

---

[10] Qu'elle.

Se divertir de la foy baptismale,
Pour ensuivir une loy faulse & male
Contrairement [11] à nostre droicte divin?
Certes ouy, dont preveu ce scandale,
Nous sommes tous bien pres de nostre fin.

L'Autheur au Lecteur.

Lecteur Chrestien, qui és fort & delivre
Et qui as faim d'ensuyvre les prudens,
Tout de nouveau j'ay composé ce livre,
Que de bon coeur je te presente & livre,
Pour te garder de plusieurs accidens.
Tu y liras les signes evidens
De l'Antechrist, filz de perdition,
Aussi la fin & consommation
De ce bas siecle, où bastir tu proposes;
Regarde-le par recreation,
Et tu verras de merveilleuses choses.

---

[11] contrainte. *Emending simply to* contraire *leaves the meter defective.*

Lightning Source UK Ltd.
Milton Keynes UK
UKHW040641051222
413345UK00005B/650